Would Rather

BOOK FOR K|DS

A HILARIOUS AND INTERACTIVE QUESTION GAME BOOK FOR KIDS

Johnny B.Good

Welcome to

Would You Rather Game Book

The would you rather game is a fun and easy little game for children of all ages to play. As long as they are old enough to comprehend the questions, of course. It keeps them entertained while challenging their brain a bit to get them thinking.

All of these questions are made for kids and with kids in mind. Some are simple. Some you may need to think a little harder on. Some may make you laugh (we hope a few will). But we do know these will keep your kids busy for awhile. And hopefully get a few giggles out of them in the process.

However, you can feel rest assured that this list is filled with clean and kid-friendly questions that will give your child hours of entertainment.

TABLE OF CONTENTS

RULES OF THE GAME

- FACE YOUR OPPONENT AND DECIDE WHO IS "PLAYER 1" AND "PLAYER 2".

- STARTING WITH 'PLAYER 1', READ THE WOULD YOU RATHER QUESTION ALOUD AND PICK THE ANSWER. THE SAME PLAYER WILL THEN EXPLAIN WHY THEY CHOSE THAT ANSWER IN THE MOST WEIRD AND HILARIOUS WAY POSSIBLE!

- IF THE REASON MAKES 'PLAYER 2' LAUGH, THEN A LAUGH POINT IS SCORED!

- TAKE TURNS GOING BACK AND FORTH, THEN MARK YOUR TOTAL LAUGH POINTS AT THE END OF EACH ROUND!

- WHOEVER GETS THE MOST LAUGH POINTS IS OFFICIALLY CROWNED THE 'LAUGH MASTER'.

- IF ENDING WITH A TIE, FINISH WITH THE TIE-BREAKER ROUND FOR WINNER TAKES ALL!

MOST IMPORTANTLY, HAVE FUN AND BE SILLY!

REMEMBER, these scenarios listed in the book are solely for fun and games! Please do NOT attempt any of the crazy scenarios in this book.

ROUND

ONE

Would you rather..

WEAR A FACE MASK WHEN YOU'RE
IN PUBLIC, AROUND PEOPLE WHO
DON'T LIVE IN YOUR HOUSEHOLD
OR
WHEN YOU ARE IN THE TOILET?

Point____

WASH YOUR HANDS WITH SOAP AND
WATER FOR 20 SECONDS
OR
WASH THEM WITH YOUR MOM'S
PERFUME?

Point____

Would you rather..

KEEP AT LEAST 6 FEET AWAY FROM
PEOPLE WHO ARE SICK
OR
STAY IN CONTACT WITH A SMELLY
SKUNK?

Point____

COVER YOUR MOUTH AND NOSE
WITH A TISSUE WHEN COUGHING
AND SNEEZING
OR
FREELY COUGH AND SNEEZE IN
FRONT OF OTHER PEOPLE?

Point____

Would you rather..

MEET AN INFECTED MICKEY MOUSE,
OR
MARY POPPINS BE REAL AND LIVING
WITH YOU?

Point____

SPEND ALL THE QUARANTINE WITH
THE TIGER SHERE KHAN
OR
SCAR THE LION?

13

Point____

Would you rather..

THROW YOUR TISSUE IN A CLOSED
GARBAGE CAN AFTER COUGHING
OR
GIFT IT TO YOUR TEACHER SO SHE
CAN THINK TO YOU EVERY TIME SHE
OPENS IT?

Point____

SHARE YOUR FACE MASK WITH YOUR
BEST FRIEND TO EXPRESS YOUR
LOVE
OR
HAVE YOUR PERSONAL FACE MASK?

Point____

Would you rather..

RUN OUT OF TOILET PAPER
OR
RUN OUT OF ALL YOUR QUARANTINE SNACKS?

Point____

BE SELF-ISOLATING WITH A CHILD WHO INSISTS ON RE-WATCHING THE SAME EPISODE OF INSIDE OUT,
OR
THE SAME EPISODE OF PADDINGTON 2?

Point____

Would you rather..

SANITIZE YOUR HANDS AFTER
TOUCHING PUBLIC SURFACES
OR
RUB THEM ON YOUR TEACHER'S
JACKET?

Point____

TOUCH YOUR EYES AND NOSE
AFTER YOU GO TO THE TOILET
(TO BE SURE THEY DIDN'T FALL
INTO)
OR
WASH AND SANITIZE YOUR HANDS?

Point____

Would you rather..

EAT ONLY GREEN VEGGIES FOR THE
REST OF THE QUARANTINE

OR

ONE GIANT ICE CREAM ONLY BUT
ONCE IN YOUR LIFE?

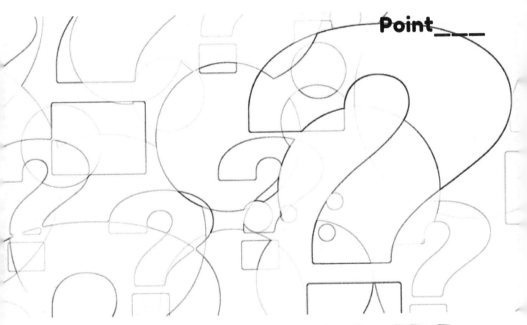

Point____

BE ISOLATING WITH ONE LITTLE
CHILD THAT WANTS TO BE
ENTERTAINED,

OR

MANY OTHER CHILDREN THAT WANT
YOU TO BREAK UP FIGHTS OVER
WHOSE TURN IT IS TO USE THE
SOUP LADLE AS A SWORD?

Point____

Would you rather..

AVOID UNNECESSARY EXPOSURE TO OTHERS, PARTICULARLY IF YOU LIVE WITH A GRANDPARENT

OR

INVITE YOUR FRIENDS AT HOME TO PLAY WITH THEM?

Point____

GO OUTSIDE TO PLAY IN THE SCHOOL YARD FOR FRESH AIR

OR

PLAY AT "BOTTOM-BURP" WITH FRIENDS IN A CLOSED SPACE?

Point____

Would you rather..

BE STUCK IN ONE ROOM WITH YOUR
FAMILY FOR A WEEK

OR

STUCK IN A ROOM BY YOURSELF
WITHOUT YOUR PHONE FOR A
WEEK?

Point____

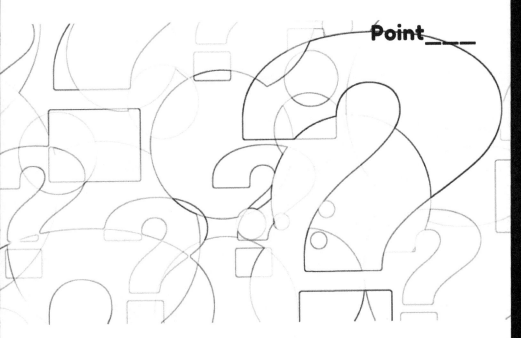

WATCH YOUR PARENTS MAKE
TIKTOK VIDEOS FOR AN ENTIRE
MONTH

OR

PLAY THE SAME BOARD GAME WITH
YOUR FAMILY EVERY DAY FOR A
MONTH.?

Point____

Would you rather..

LICK YOUR FINGERS AFTER PLAYING
BASKETBALL
OR
FOLLOW YOUR MOM'S SUGGESTION
TO WASH THEM?

Point____

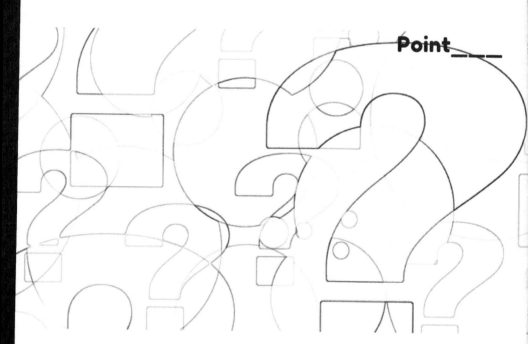

WEARING GLOVES WHEN YOU HAVE
TO TOUCH SOMETHING RISKY
OR
COVER YOUR HANDS WITH YOUR
DIRTY SOCKS?

Point____

Would you rather..

REMOVE THE GLOVES YOU USED
BEFORE AS SOON AS YOU GET IN
YOUR DAD'S CAR

OR

KEEP THEM ON, TOUCH EVERYTHING
AND USE YOUR DIRTY SOCKS AS AN
AIR FRESHENER?

Point____

WEAR YOUR FACE MASK COVERING
NOSE AND MOUTH

OR

LEAVE YOUR NOSE UNCOVERED SO
TO SMELL BETTER YOUR FRIEND'S
FEET?

Point____

Would you rather..

CONTRACT A DANGEROUS ILLNESS
(AND SURVIVE)
OR
SPEND A WEEK WITH NO SHOWER?

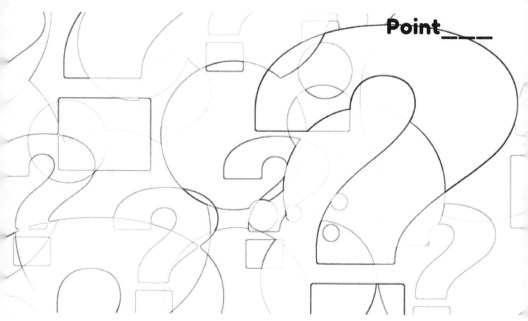

Point____

YOU'RE ALL OUT OF FOOD....

would you rather

EAT POOP FLAVORED CHOCOLATE
OR
CHOCOLATE FLAVORED POOP?

Point____

Would you rather..

SHARE TOWELS WITH YOUR FAMILY, FRIENDS, AND ANIMALS
OR
AVOID SHARING THEM IN ORDER TO LIMIT THE SPREAD OF A DANGEROUS VIRUS?

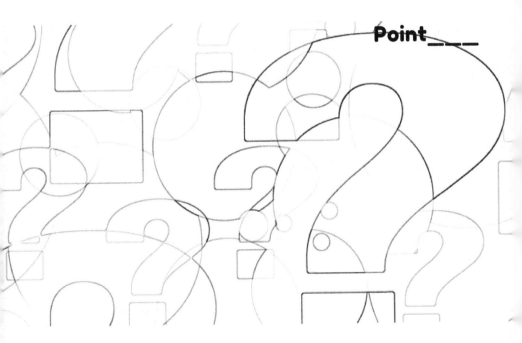

Point____

WASH YOUR HANDS FREQUENTLY
OR
JUST ONCE A WEEK?

Point____

Would you rather..

RINSE THOROUGHLY WITH RUNNING WATER
OR
WAIT FOR THE RAIN SO TO WASH THEM BETTER?

Point____

SHARE WHAT YOU LEARN ABOUT PREVENTING DISEASE WITH YOUR FAMILY AND FRIENDS, ESPECIALLY WITH YOUNGER CHILDREN
OR
SHARE YOUR BIRTHDAY PRESENT WITH THEM?

Point____

Would you rather..

RINSE THOROUGHLY WITH RUNNING
WATER
OR
WAIT FOR THE RAIN SO TO WASH
THEM BETTER?

Point____

TELL YOUR TEACHER IF YOU FEEL
SICK
OR
REMAIN SILENT UNTIL EVERYONE
GETS SICK?

25

Point____

Would you rather..

BE OUT OF TOILET PAPER
OR
A HAND SANITIZER GEL?

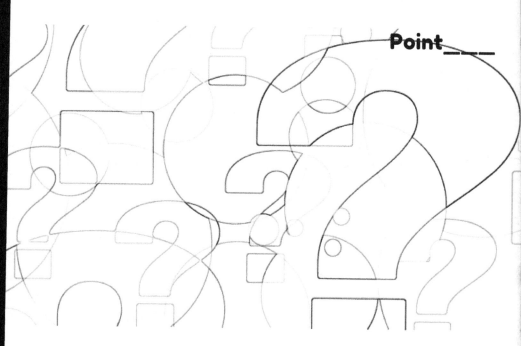

Point_____

BE QUARANTINED WITH GOOD
INTERNET BUT NO VIDEO GAMES
OR
NO INTERNET BUT ACCESS TO ALL
VIDEO GAMES PRIOR TO 2020?

Point_____

Would you rather..

REACH OUT TO FRIENDS AFTER
SCHOOL VIA PHONE/VIDEO CHATS
OR
HANGOUT WITH THEM AT THEIR
HOME BUT IN TWO DIFFERENT
ROOMS?

Point_____

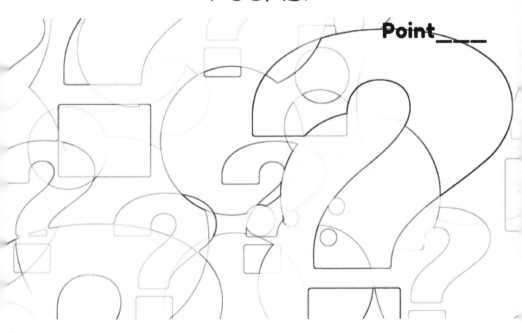

WATCH A NEW MOVIE AT HOME
OR
GO TO THE CINEMA FULL OF PEOPLE
DRESSED IN FACE-MASK, GLOVES
AND A SKI SUIT?

Point_____

Would you rather..

OPEN THE CLASSROOM DOOR,
BRINGING IN THE DOORKNOB WITH
YOUR TEETH

OR

LEAVE THE CLASSROOM DOOR
OPENED TO HELP REDUCE HIGH
TOUCH SURFACES?

Point____

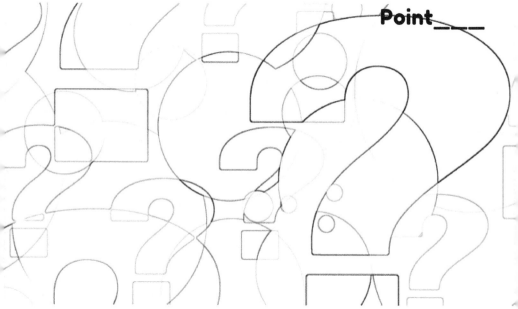

USE THE SEAT ASSIGNED TO YOU
BY THE BUS RIDER

OR

SIT ON THE DRIVER'S SEAT AND
DRIVE THE BUS TO GO TO SCHOOL?

28

Point____

Would you rather..

BE STUCK INSIDE WITH VIDEO GAMES
BUT NO BATHROOM
OR
NO VIDEO GAMES OUTSIDE BY AN
OUTHOUSE?

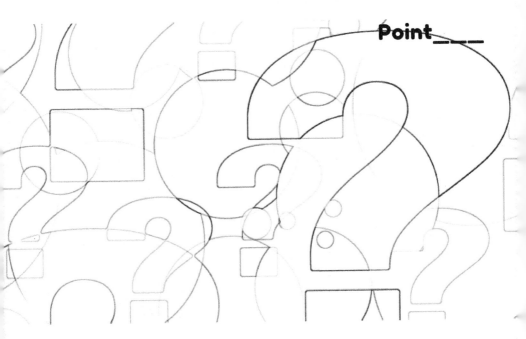

Point____

BE QUARANTINED AT YOUR HOUSE
ALL YEAR BUT BE ABLE TO HAVE
FRIENDS OVER
OR
HAVE SCHOOL ALL YEAR ROUND?

Point____

Would you rather..

FOLLOW THE ONE-WAY ARROWS TO
GO INTO YOUR CLASS WHEN YOU
ARE AT SCHOOL
OR
GO INTO YOUR CLASS WITH YOUR
SKATEBOARD?

Point____

SAY HELLO TO YOUR FRIEND ASKING
HIM FOR A "HIGH FIVE" (OR A BIG
HUG)
OR
SAY "HELLO" WHILE KEEPING THE
RIGHT DISTANCE?

Point____

ROUND

TWO

Would you rather..

HAVE ENOUGH SPACE BETWEEN
YOUR SCHOOL DESK AND THAT OF
YOUR FRIEND
OR
PUT ONE DESK UPON ANOTHER ONE
TO BETTER SEE THE BLACKBOARD?

Point____

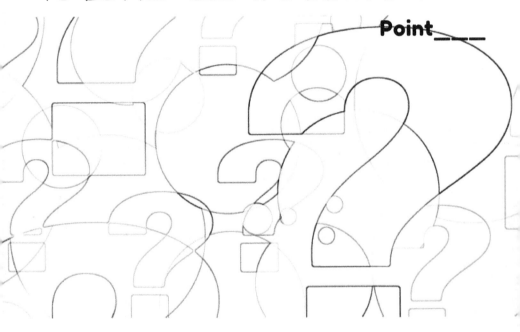

USE A RESEALABLE BAG TO STORE
THE MASK WHEN YOU CAN'T WEAR
IT
OR
KEEP IT INSIDE THE SCIENCE BOOK?

Point____

Would you rather..

WATCH ONLY FROZEN 2
OR
TANGLED FOR THE REST OF
QUARANTINE?

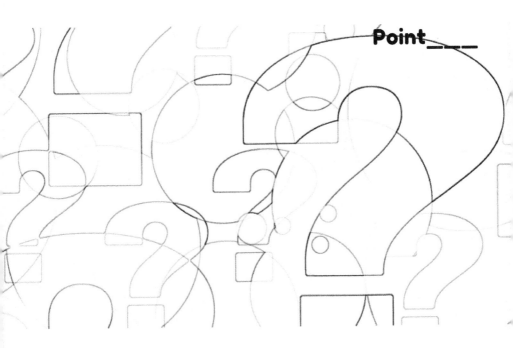

Point____

LIVE OFF ONLY CANNED MEATS
OR
CANNED VEGETABLES?

Point____

Would you rather..

DRY YOUR HANDS WITH A CLEAN,
DRY CLOTH, SINGLE-USE TOWEL
OR
DRY THEM ON YOUR FRIEND'S
JACKET?

Point____

EAT YOUR MEAL AT YOUR DESK
OR
PLAY "FOOD FIGHT" WITH YOUR
SCHOOL MATES?

Point____

Would you rather..

TAKE A SELFIE ON A PUBLIC
RESTROOM TOILET SEAT
OR
PLAY A GAME OF TAG WITH YOUR
FRIEND WHO HAS THE MEASLES?

Point____

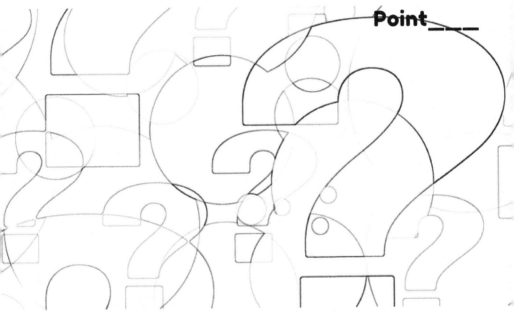

YOU ARE ALL OUT OF TOILET PAPER,

Would You Rather...

WIPE WITH A LEAF THAT MIGHT BE
POISON IVY,
OR
A PINECONE?

37

Point____

Would you rather..

REMOVE THE FACE MASK(OR PUT ONE ON) HANDLING THE EAR LOOPS
OR
WEAR A PAIR OF UNDERWEAR FOR A CAP?

Point____

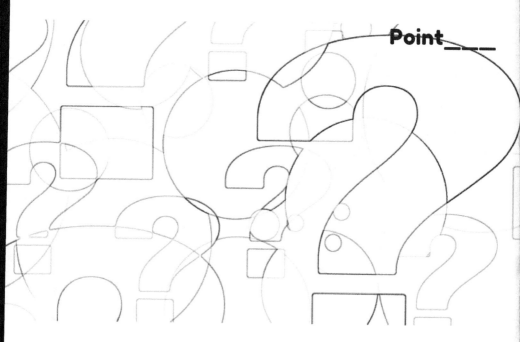

WEAR A FACE MASK EVERY TIME YOU ARE IN PUBLIC
OR
JUST FOR HALLOWEEN AND CARNIVAL?

Point____

Would you rather..

SHARE YOUR ROOM WITH A SICK
HARRY POTTER

OR

SHARE YOUR ROOM WITH ANGRY
JACK SPARROW?

Point____

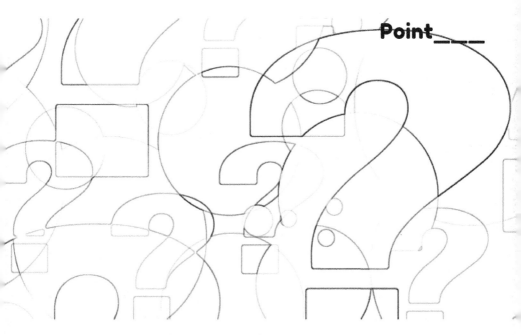

SCRUB ALL SURFACES OF THE
HANDS – INCLUDING BACKS OF
HANDS, BETWEEN FINGERS AND
UNDER NAILS – FOR AT LEAST 20
SECONDS

OR

WASH YOURSELF WITH A FIRE
EXTINGUISHER?

Point____

Would you rather..

BE QUARANTINED WITH BIGFOOT
OR
A MERMAID?

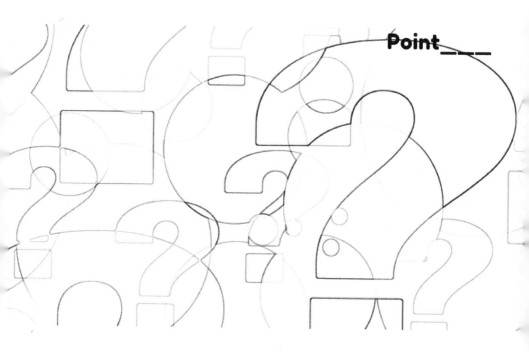

Point____

BE QUARANTINED AT HOME FOR A
WEEK
OR
STUDY MATH FOR 2 DAYS?

Point____

Would you rather..

BE AS LITTLE AS VIRUS
OR
BIG LIKE A HIPPO?

Point_____

HAVE A PIG'S SNOUTS
OR
ELEPHANT EARS?

Point_____

Would you rather..

HAVE DIARRHEA FOR 2 WEEKS
OR
HAVE TO STAY IN ISOLATION
FOREVER?

Point____

LOOK SKINNY AND BE STRONG
OR
LOOK BIG AND BE WEAK?

Point____

Would you rather..

LOSE YOUR FREEDOM BUT BE SAFE
OR
TAKE A CONTAGIOUS DISEASE AND
BE FREE?

Point____

WEAR A FACE MASK WHENEVER YOU
ARE IN PUBLIC
OR
A GIANT RED CLOWN NOSE THAT
PEOPLE KEEP SQUEAKING?

Point____

Would you rather..

CLEAN YOUR HANDS BEFORE AND AFTER TOUCHING YOUR MASK.
OR
GET A NEW MASK EVERY TIME AND KEEP YOUR HANDS DIRTY?

Point____

TAKE OFF CLOTH FACE MASKS TO AVOID TOUCHING THE CLOTH PORTIONS
OR
WEAR AN IRON MASK FOR THE REST OF YOUR LIFE?

44   **Point____**

Would you rather..

SHARE OR TRADE STICKERS WITH OTHERS

OR

NOT SHARE ANYTHING TO AVOID CONTAGION?

Point____

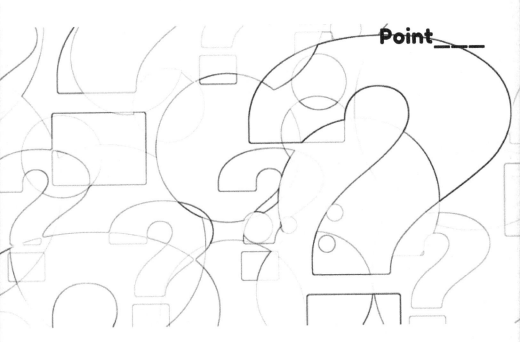

MAKE DAILY TEMPERATURE READINGS AS A PART OF ACTUAL SYMPTOM SCREENING

OR

READING A BOOK A DAY FOR THE REST OF YOUR LIFE?

Point____

Would you rather..

TELL BAD JOKES AND MAKE EVERYONE GROAN FOR AN HOUR EVERY DAY,

OR

LISTEN TO SOMEONE TELLING BAD JOKES FOR AN HOUR EVERY DAY?

Point____

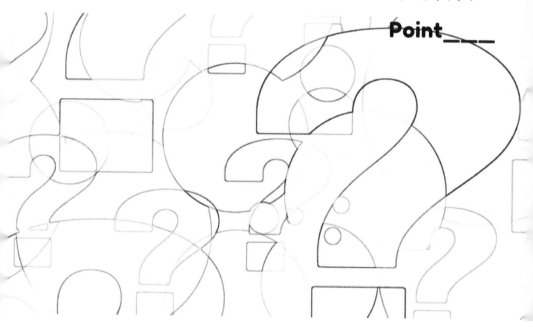

GROW AN EXTRA SET OF EARS, BUT NOT HEAR VERY WELL,

OR

AN EXTRA TONGUE BUT NOT TASTE VERY WELL?

Point____

Would you rather..

EAT A LARGE CAN OF DOG FOOD
OR
A LARGE PLATE OF CAULIFLOWER?

Point____

SCRUB THE WASHROOM FLOOR
WITH YOUR TOOTHBRUSH FOR AN
ENTIRE DAY,
OR
CLEAN YOUR TEETH WITH A
TOOTHBRUSH SOMEONE ELSE HAS
USED IN THEIR MOUTH?

47

Point____

Would you rather..

EAT FOOD THAT TASTES GOOD BUT LOOKS LIKE POOP,
OR
FOOD THAT LOOKS GOOD BUT TASTES LIKE POOP?

Point____

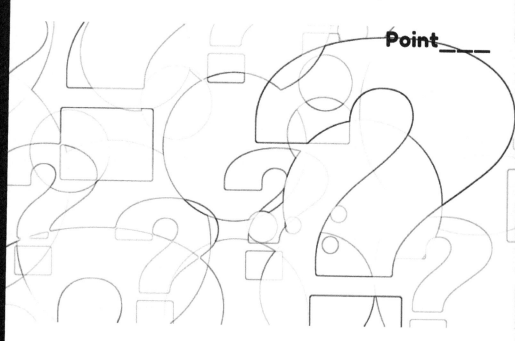

SPEND A WEEK WEARING A DIFFERENT STRANGER'S DIRTY CLOTHES EVERY DAY,
OR
WEAR YOUR OWN CLOTHES, BUT YOU CANNOT CHANGE THEM FOR ONE YEAR?

Point____

Would you rather..

USE SHAMPOO TO BRUSH YOUR TEETH
OR
TOOTHPASTE TO WASH YOUR HAIR?

Point____

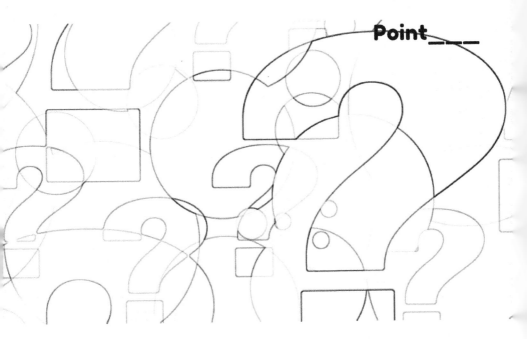

MAINTAIN A DISTANCE OF AT LEAST 3 FEET BETWEEN EVERYONE PRESENT AT SCHOOL
OR
MAINTAIN A DISTANCE OF AT LEAST 3 MILES BETWEEN YOU AND THE SCHOOL?

Point____

Would you rather..

RESPECT THE USE OF SIGNS, GROUND MARKINGS, TAPE, BARRIERS AND OTHER MEANS TO AVOID CONTAGION

OR

PLAY PARKOUR WITH THEM?

Point____

ENCOURAGE SCHOOL MATES NOT TO GATHER AND SOCIALIZE IN BIG GROUPS UPON LEAVING SCHOOL GROUNDS

OR

PLAY THE "HUMAN PYRAMID" ALL TOGETHER?

Point____

Would you rather..

RESPECT PHYSICAL DISTANCING
MEASURES DURING LUNCH BREAKS
OR
GO OUT TO EAT AT THE
RESTAURANT ALL TOGETHER?

Point____

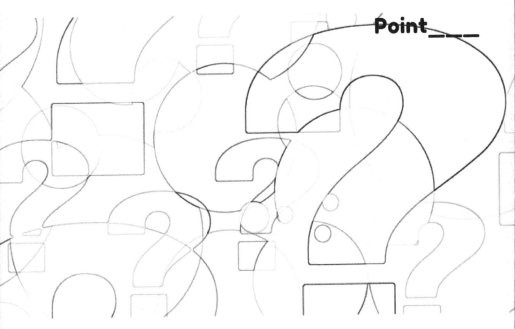

IMMEDIATELY ASK TO CLEAN
SURFACES AND OBJECTS THAT ARE
VISIBLY SOILED
OR
PLAY "THE HUMAN STICKER" ON
THEM TO REMOVE BACTERIA FROM
YOUR BODY?

Point____

Would you rather..

SPEND A WEEK WITH A SICK BATMAN
OR
SPEND A DAY WITH AN INSANE JOKER?

Point____

SPEND A WEEK WEARING A DIFFERENT STRANGER'S DIRTY CLOTHES EVERY DAY,
OR
WEAR YOUR OWN CLOTHES, BUT YOU CANNOT CHANGE THEM FOR ONE YEAR?

Point____

ROUND

THREE

Would you rather..

WEAR SEE-THROUGH CLOTHES,
OR
HAVE EVERYONE YOU KNOW WEAR
SEE-THROUGH CLOTHES?

Point____

DO A LOUD FART AND HAVE
EVERYONE KNOW YOU DID IT,
OR
A REALLY STINKY ONE AND HAVE
NOBODY KNOW?

Point____

Would you rather..

BE TRAPPED IN A ROOM WITH 30
SCREAMING BABIES
OR
A DANGEROUS VIRUS?

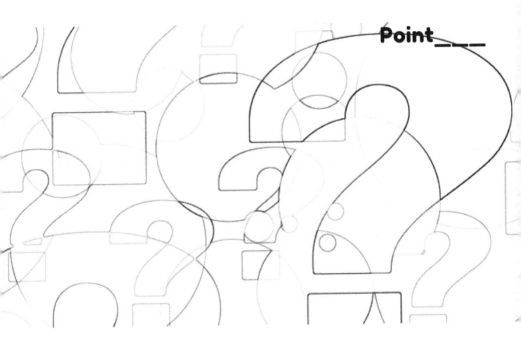

Point____

TAKE A BATH IN ICE CUBES,
OR
TAKE A BATH IN TOMATO SOUP?

Point____

Would you rather..

GET SICK IMMEDIATELY BEFORE A
SCHOOL TEST AND STAY AT HOME
WHEN YOUR FRIENDS PLAY OUTSIDE
OR
GO TO SCHOOL AND PLAY WITH
FRIENDS LATER?

Point____

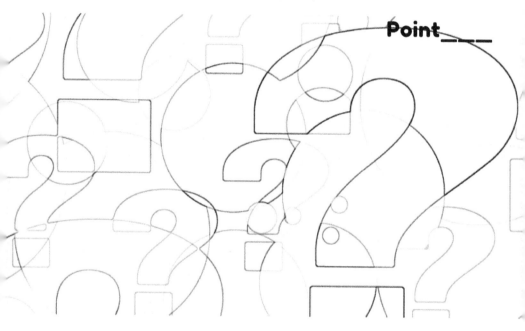

ESCAPE THE PANDEMIC BY LIVING
UNDERGROUND FOREVER,
OR
IN SPACE FOREVER?

Point____

Would you rather..

KNOW THE DATE OF THE END OF
THE PANDEMIC
OR
KNOW ITS CAUSE?

Point____

STAY CLOSED IN YOUR HOUSE
WAITING FOR THE END OF PANDEMIC,
OR
GO OUT AND FIND A SOLUTION TO
FIGHT AGAINST IT?

Point____

Would you rather..

TOUCH THE RAILING WHILE WALKING
UP AND DOWN THE STAIRS
OR
NOT TOUCH IT AT ALL?

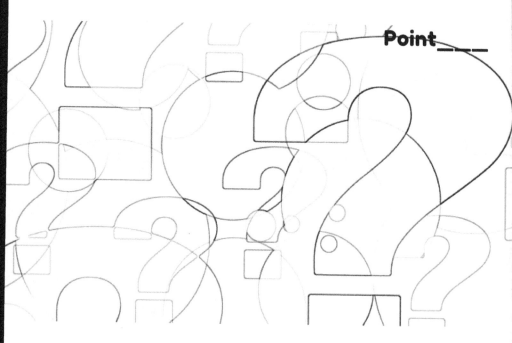

Point____

KEEP THE CLASSROOM DOORS
OPEN TO AVOID TOUCHING DOOR-
KNOBS
OR
PASS THROUGH IT WITH A NINJA
KICK?

Point____

Would you rather..

STAY HOME AND SELF-ISOLATE IF YOU SHOULD FEEL ILL
OR
NOT TELL ANYONE AND GO TO THE PARK TO PLAY WITH YOUR FRIENDS?

Point____

CREATE FUN POSTERS THAT CAN BE HUNG IN THE HALLWAYS TO REMIND OTHERS TO STICK TO THE SANITATION RULES
OR
DESIGN GRAFFITI OF YOUR FAVORITE SUPER HEROES?

Point____

Would you rather..

TOUCH YOUR MOUTH, NOSE OR EYES, AFTER TOUCHING SURFACES CONTAMINATED WITH BACTERIA
OR
SANITIZE YOUR HANDS WITH A STINKY HAND-SANITIZER?

Point____

BE QUARANTINED WITH YOUR TEACHER
OR
WITH YOUR OBNOXIOUS ENEMY?

Point____

Would you rather..

LEARN A NEW CRAFT,
OR
LIE ON THE COUCH AND STARE AT
THE UNDONE HOMEWORK?

Point____

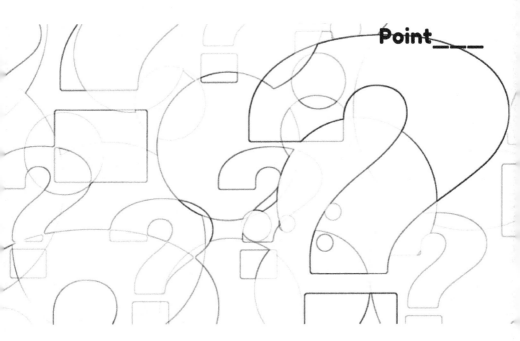

GIVE YOUR LITTLE SISTER YOUR
PASSWORD TO DOWNLOAD GAMES
ON YOUR PHONE ONLY TO FIND YOU
HAVE PAID $1283 IN BARBIE GAME
EXTRAS,
OR
HAVE TO PLAY WITH ACTUAL
BARBIES 17 HOURS A DAY?

Point____

Would you rather..

SCREAM TO A GROUP OF BULLIES
THAT ARE NO WEARING FACE MASKS
AND RISK BEING CHASED,
OR
SAY NOTHING AND RISK THEY WILL
BE INFECTED?

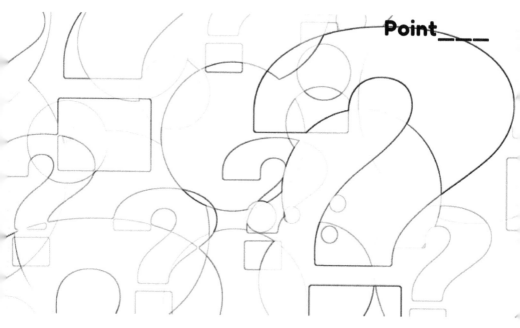

Point____

SPEND THE REST OF YOUR LIFE
ONLY SPEAKING IN RHYME,
OR
NOT SAY ANYTHING FOR ONE
YEAR??

Point____

Would you rather..

HAVE SOMEONE CATCH YOU PICKING
YOUR NOSE AND EATING IT,
OR
SCRATCHING YOUR BUM AND
SNIFFING YOUR FINGERS?

Point____

TRY TO GO TO THE WASHROOM ON
A TINY TOILET THAT WILL OVERFLOW
OR
A GIANT TOILET YOU MIGHT FALL
INTO?

Point____

Would you rather..

KEEP ONE INFECTED DOLLAR YOU
FOUND ON THE GROUND
OR
RECEIVE A KISS FROM A
TOOTHLESS OLD WOMAN?

Point____

HAVE ONE EYE IN THE MIDDLE OF
YOUR HEAD
OR
TWO NOSES?

Point____

Would you rather..

BE STUCK IN QUARANTINE WITH
SPONGEBOB
OR
HARRY POTTER?

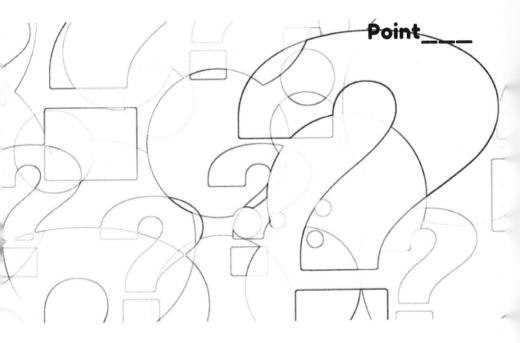

Point____

BE STUCK IN A HOUSE FULL OF
SPIDERS
OR
BACTERIA?

Point____

Would you rather..

LIVE WITHOUT CHOCOLATE ALL
YOUR LIFE
OR
LIVE WITHOUT YOUR IPAD FOR ONE
MONTH?

Point____

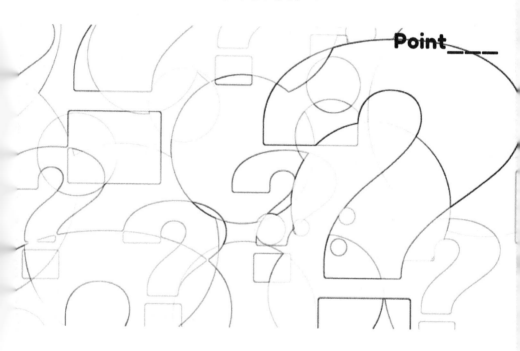

BE AN UNKNOWN SUPERHERO
OR
A FAMOUS VILLAIN?

Point____

Would you rather..

GO TO THE DOCTOR
OR
TO THE DENTIST?

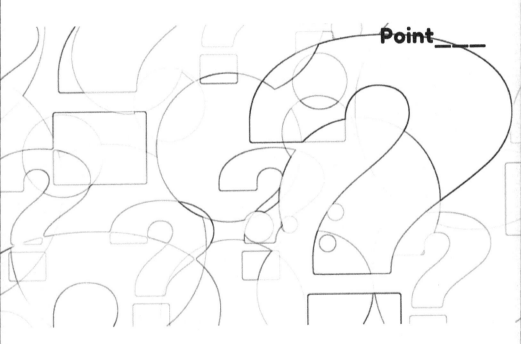

Point____

BE STUCK IN QUARANTINE WITH
DRACULA
OR
A DANGEROUS VIRUS?

Point____

Would you rather..

HAVE A PIG NOSE
OR
A MONKEY FACE?

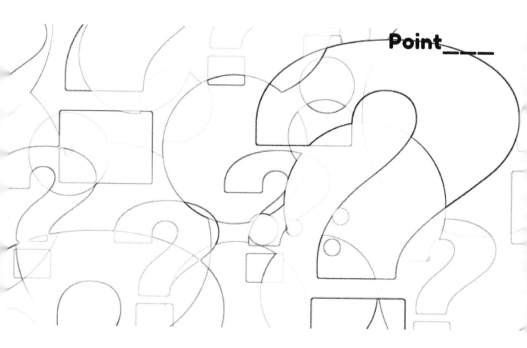

Point____

BE ABLE TO READ MINDS
OR
SEE ONE DAY INTO THE FUTURE?

Point____

Would you rather..

BE STUCK IN QUARANTINE FOREVER
OR
LIVE NORMALLY BUT GET SICK
EVERY MONTH?

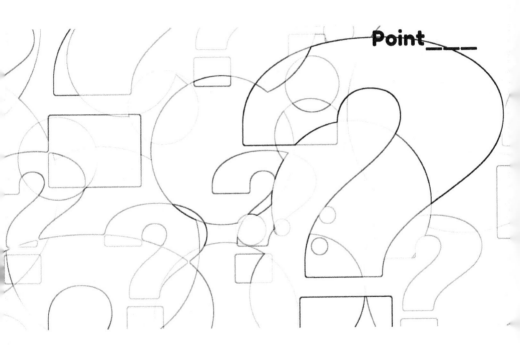

Point_____

HAVE REALLY SMALL HANDS
OR
REALLY BIG FEET?

Point_____

Would you rather..

FART REALLY LOUD
OR
POOP YOUR PANTS SILENTLY?

Point____

USE EYE DROPS MADE OF VINEGAR
OR
TOILET PAPER MADE FROM
SANDPAPER?

Point____

THE

END

I hope you enjoyed this book!

This is a fun and simple way to keep your children informed.

Knowing the facts is key to being properly prepared and protecting yourself and your loved ones.

If you think that this book has been helpful, please, <u>leave a review</u> and help other customers make the right choice...

Thank You!

Printed in Great Britain
by Amazon